Dinosaur Duel

by Monica Hughes

Consultant: Dougal Dixon

CONTENTS

Words in **bold** are explained in the glossary.

Fighting dinosaurs

Some dinosaurs did a lot of fighting.

Some dinosaurs fought using their hard heads to hit each other.

This dinosaur hit out with its big claws.

Dinosaurs that liked to eat meat

Meat-eating dinosaurs ate other dinosaurs.

Dilophosaurus was a small dinosaur that ate meat. It ran very fast to catch its food.

Dilophosaurus
dil-o-fo-sor-us

T. rex had a huge mouth and lots of teeth. It could fit a small dinosaur in its mouth.

Tyrannosaurus rex
tie-ran-o-sor-us rex

Allosaurus

Allosaurus was one of the biggest meat-eating dinosaurs.

It was big and strong and good at fighting.

It had big claws and about 70 big teeth.

It could kill big plant-eating dinosaurs.

Allosaurus
al-o-sor-us

Small killer dinosaurs

Not all meat-eating dinosaurs were big.

Deinonychus
die-non-ee-cus

Deinonychus was small but it hunted in a **pack** with others.

This made it easier for them to kill a big dinosaur.

Dinosaurs that liked to eat plants

Some plant-eating
dinosaurs were very tall.
Some were very long.
Some were both!

The tall ones could reach
up to the tops of trees.

Seismosaurus
size-mo-sor-us

Many plant-eating dinosaurs were too big for meat-eaters to **attack**.

Sauroposeidon
saw-ro-po-si-don

Heterodontosaurus

This plant-eating dinosaur ran very fast.

It also looked very scary.

So some meat-eating dinosaurs ran away from it.

It was saved from being eaten!

Heterodontosaurus
het-er-o-don-to-saw-rus

Horns and spikes

Some plant-eating dinosaurs had to fight meat-eating dinosaurs.

They had horns or spikes to stop the meat-eating dinosaurs killing them.

Sauropelta
sor-o-pel-ta

Triceratops was a dinosaur
with three horns on its head.

Triceratops
try-serra-tops

Spikes

Sauropelta had
spikes on its neck.

Plates

Some plant-eating dinosaurs had plates on their backs to protect them from attack.

This dinosaur had small plates over its back and tail.

This dinosaur had two rows of plates down its back and tail.

Plates

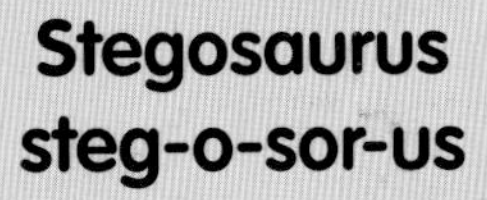

Armour and clubs

Euoplocephalus
you-o-plo-seffa-lus

Armour

Some plant-eating dinosaurs had **armour**.

Some had a tail with
a club on the end.

They could hit a meat-eating
dinosaur with the club.

This dinosaur had armour
and a **tail club**, too.

Glossary

armour
A hard covering that protects the body.

pack
A group of animals that come together to hunt.

plates

Hard, flat bones that often stick out from the back.

T. rex

A large, fierce meat-eating dinosaur.

tail club

A hard, bony tail tip used to hit attackers.

Index

First published in Great Britain in 2008 by **ticktock Media Ltd.,**
Unit 2, Orchard Business Centre, North Farm Road, Tunbridge Wells, Kent TN2 3XF
ISBN 978 1 84696 768 9 pbk
Printed in China

A CIP catalogue record for this book is available from the British Library.

We would like to thank: Penny Worms, Shirley Bickler, Suzanne Baker and the National Literacy Trust.

Picture credits (t=top, b=bottom, c=centre, l-left, r=right, OFC= outside front cover)
Lisa Alderson: 13, 16-17, 23t; John Alston: 7t, 6b, 8b; Simon Mendez: 17tr, 19, 23b; Natural History Museum: 12, 21; Luis Rey: 1, 4, 5, 10-11, 15, 18, 20, 22t, 22b, 23r; Science Photo Library: 9; Shutterstock: 7b, 23c.

Every effort has been made to trace the copyright holders, and we apologise in advance for any unintentional omissions. We would be pleased to insert the appropriate acknowledgements in any subsequent edition of this publication.